Preston Primary
School

SHARKS

Andrew Solway

OXFORD
UNIVERSITY PRESS

Contents

Introduction

What is that black fin in the water? Is it a shark?

This book tells you all about sharks.
It tells you what they look like, what they eat and where they live.

Tails and fins

A shark is a fish.

gills

tail fin

fins

A shark has a tail and fins for swimming, just like other fishes.

eye

A shark's skin is covered in scales that look like tiny 'teeth'.

snout

Sharks breathe through their gills.

Kinds of sharks

There are hundreds of different sharks.

great white

hammerhead

carpet shark

Some sharks live far out in the ocean.
Some live near the shore.

whale shark

cookie-cutter shark

A whale shark is very big. It is bigger than a bus!
A cookie-cutter shark is small. It is smaller than a
dinner plate.

Fierce hunters

Most sharks are fierce hunters.

8

The great white shark is the biggest hunter in the sea. It hunts seals and penguins. It hunts other sharks too.

This dolphin has been bitten by a cookie-cutter shark.

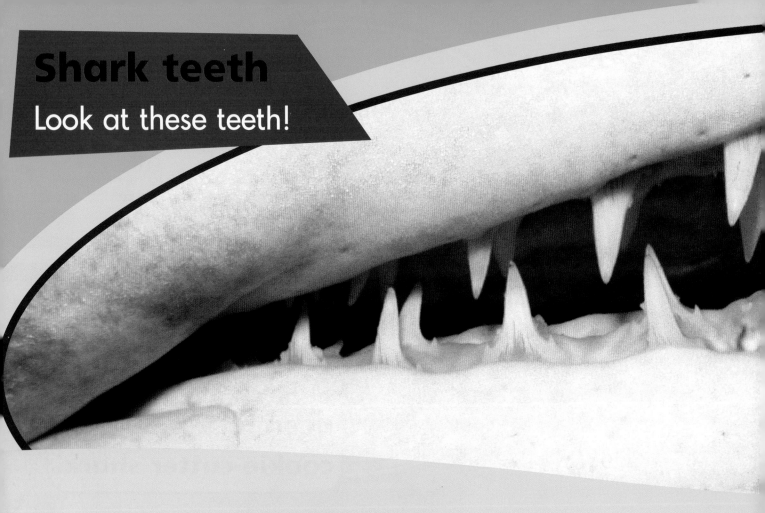

Look at these teeth!

10 There are hundreds of them!
They are very sharp and pointed.

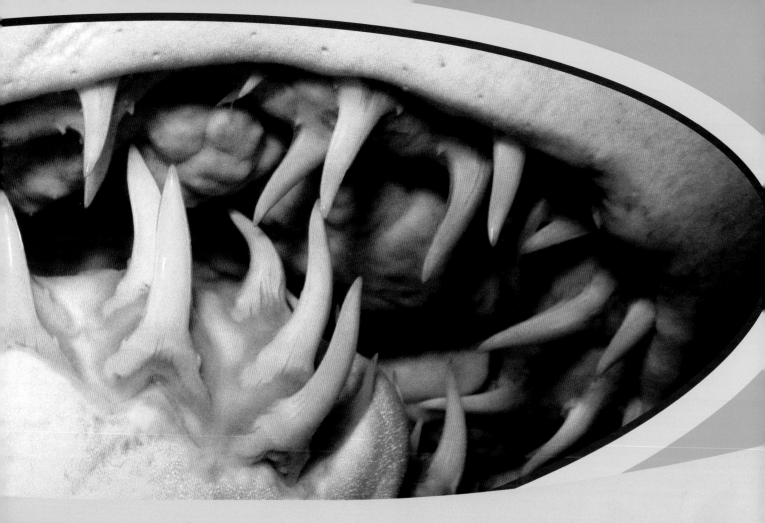

When a tooth wears out, a new one grows
to take its place.

Fast and strong

Sharks are very strong and they can swim very fast.

12 Shark bodies are long and smooth. The shape helps them to slide easily through the water.

Sometimes thresher sharks jump right out of the water!

Sharp senses

Sharks have sharp senses. They use their senses to hunt their food.

They can smell food.
They can feel movement in the water so they know when other fishes are near.

14

This hammerhead shark is hunting other fishes.

Eggs and babies

Most fishes lay eggs in the water. The eggs hatch out into baby fishes.

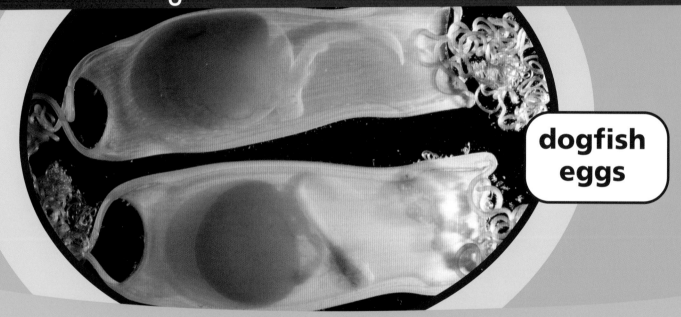

dogfish eggs

This dogfish shark lays eggs like other fishes, but most sharks have live babies.

16

This is a new baby lemon shark.

Harmless sharks

Not all sharks are fierce.

Basking shark

The biggest sharks are whale sharks and basking sharks.

Whale shark

They have huge mouths but they are both harmless. They eat tiny plankton.

Carpet sharks

Carpet sharks lie on the sea bed.

They look like rocks.

Carpet sharks live in warm, shallow seas.

They wait for small fishes to swim past.
Then – snap! They eat them up.

Now you know

So now you know about sharks.

- Sharks are fishes.
- There are hundreds of different kinds.
- Most sharks are fierce hunters, but some are harmless. A few are gentle giants.
- They can be bigger than buses, or as small as a plate.

22 What else do you remember about them?

Index